# 28 Day *Creating Characters* Challenge

## M.H. Salter

Daytime Moon Publishing

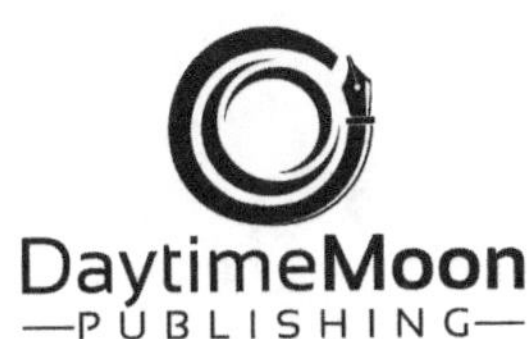

*Others In This Series by M.H. Salter*

28 Day *Novel Writing* Challenge
28 Day *Story Structure* Challenge
28 Day *First Chapter* Challenge
28 Day *Endings* Challenge

*

*Fiction Books by M.H. Salter*

Doorways
Dove
A Rose By Any Other Name

*

*Non-Fiction Books by M.H. Salter*

Peter Tork: Words of Wisdom From A.A. to ZEN
Davy Jones: Words of Wisdom From A.A. to ZEN

# Introduction

Hello, Writer!

Welcome to this 28 Day Challenge for writers struggling with character development.

By working through the daily lessons and writing exercises around character types, reader connection, character transformation, and glow-ups, you can bring your characters onto the page as bright and shiny as you always imagined them to be.

Aside from the physical act of writing, this challenge has a second purpose. One that is even more important. It is designed to inspire and motivate you and, most importantly, increase your belief in yourself as an artist. If you don't already consider yourself a "writer" or an "artist", then I have news for you: the fact that you are either considering this challenge — or have already signed up for it — proves that you *are* a writer because you are aiming to improve on your craft. That in itself shows that you consider yourself, and your artistic merits to be worthy.

According to science, it takes an average of 21 days to form a new habit by implementing a daily practice. It takes a following 90 days to make it into a permanent lifestyle change. This 28 Day Challenge is designed to help you incorporate writing time into your life in order for it to become routine. Over these 28 days you will learn to make yourself and your writing a priority, carve out a daily routine that can become a habit, and lead you toward a MS of which you will be proud and excited to put out into the waiting world.

In the *Creating Characters* Challenge, you will receive a daily lesson focusing on a different aspect of Character Development:

- the different character types — protagonist, antagonist, ally and the narrator — how to work with character stereotypes, and how to weave all the different character relationships together
- increasing the reader connection to your characters by analysing their core values, their shadow sides, and their false beliefs, as well as enhancing the emotional connection with writing techniques, and internal conflict.
- the character transformation arc, and the different stages through which every character needs to go

- how to give your character a "glow-up" by turning up the shine on their three-dimensional qualities, their personal stakes, their introduction to the reader, making memorable moments, and strengthening the narrative voice

- and getting excited and staying excited about your work-in-progress

So many of us will start a project, get about a third of the way through, and stop. I believe writing a novel is a cumulative process. You need to gather enough momentum (ie. excitement) at the beginning, so that when you hit those downhill slumps of self-doubt and writer's block, you will have enough inertia to get you through to actually completing your first draft. Each of these 28 day writing challenges will help you to get — and *stay* — excited about your work-in-progress.

Each daily practice contains simple, bite-sized snippets and exercises that you can either ponder on for the day and make some notes before bed, or just do in a few minutes over your morning coffee, so that even those of us who *can't* find time to write can still get something out of it. At the end of the 28 days, even if you only spent ten minutes per day on a challenge, you will end up with *four and a half hours* of writing time that you wouldn't have completed ordinarily. If you only manage a hundred words a day, by the end of the challenge you'll be *2,800 words down*! That's basically a chapter a month if you keep it up.

Remember, with this challenge, you will only get out what you put in. Allow yourself just ten minutes a day. Invest in yourself.

These daily lessons and exercises are taken from my book: *The Excited Writer*. Once this challenge is complete, you are invited to purchase the full book for even more lessons and exercises, take up another 28 Day Challenge in a specific area, or even opt to work with me one-on-one via an assessment or mentorship.

Remember, a habit takes an average of 21 days to form, and a following 90 days to become a permanent lifestyle change. Whether you finish one 28 day course and start another right away, or just continue on your own, please keep up the daily routine — even just ten minutes a day — because you are worth it.

So let's give the reader a reason to care about your characters — all of them. Show us they are human. They make mistakes. They want to be better. They hope. Your job is to make the reader *care*. And then, don't relax that grip-hold on your reader's heart.

This challenge may not have you completing your novel in 28 days, that is not the point of it. The point, my friend, is to carve out for you a new daily habit. I am honoured to be a part of your personal writing journey. Thank you for including me on the ride!

Warm regards,
Melanie Hyland Salter
(M.H. Salter)

# Day One: Character Types

The main types of characters we are going to look at this week are the protagonist (good guy), the antagonist (bad guy), and the ally (the inspirational guy).

But before we dive into the skin and bones of those three specific types, we are going to look at what all characters have that draws in a reader. What makes them interesting and relatable?

Flaws.
Wants (physical goal).
Needs (emotional goal).

These three things make up the bones of your character's journey.

First of all, let's look at the theme of your book, because everything follows on from this.

Theme is what people really mean when they say, 'Oh, you're writing a book? Cool! What's it *about*?'

The real answer to this question has nothing to do with genre or plot lines. It has to do with the ultimate *lesson* all the characters (and the reader) will learn. It has to do with a universal core value.

An example of a core value is self-worth, self-love, freedom, integrity, compassion, creativity, security, honesty, spirituality. The list could go on and on.

If your book has a strong theme based on a core value then it has resonating potential to a high volume of readers.

NOTE: Theme is a powerful tool for any writer, as it also comes with the ability — if harnessed correctly — to avoid long battles with writers block, or the dreaded "sagging middle" syndrome. If you can use your theme in every single scene you write, this will then give *every single scene* you write a *reason* to be included in the book. It will give you something to focus on when you are stuck. It will keep your book on the right path without wandering off aimlessly for a few chapters.

The theme of your book, is also your character's *need*.

While theme is unchanging in your book, the way your characters relate to this will vary between the types of characters. Why? Because each character will have a unique flaw that can only be healed by learning the lesson of the theme.

Having flaws makes them human, because nobody is perfect. Having flaws also provides them with a character arc, because it is the innate desire to heal this flaw that creates the whole point of your book.

Which brings us to the desire. There will be something that your character *wants* at the start of your book. This is the thing that they believe will solve their problem and heal their flaw.

But it won't.

For example, if your theme is self-love, and your character flaw is lack of confidence, their "want" may be finding love, or external validation through another character. But this will only be a bandaid over the actual problem of lack, and what they actually need to learn is self-love.

<u>**Exercise: 15 min**</u>

1.  First, let's work out your theme (which is also your character's *need* or emotional goal).

    Question: Oh, you're writing a book? Cool! What's it about? No… What is it *really* about? What is the core value within your story? What life lesson do your characters *need* to learn?

    Theme: _______________________________________

2.  What *flaw* does your character have that needs to be healed by the theme? In other words: what is the *opposite* of your theme? How can you turn this abstract concept into something physical?

    For example, if your theme (need) is *self-love*, the opposite of this would be *self-hatred*, and your character's flaw may therefore be *depression* or *lack of confidence*.

    Opposite of theme: _______________________________

    Internal flaw:___________________________________

3.  And from there, we can work out your character's *want* (or physical goal).

    What could be a physical and tangible solution to overcoming their internal flaw? Something that exists in the external world that they believe will fix them (but won't)?

    For example, if your character's need is *self-love,* and the internal flaw is *depression,* then a physical goal for them to *want* might be someone that showers them with affection. (But they will then realise that they can't be truly loved until they love themselves).

    External Solution: _______________________________

4.  Repeat steps TWO and THREE for all your main characters (keep the theme / need the same for each one).

# Day Two: Protagonist

The protagonist is the good guy. The hero. The one that your reader roots for and loves. The emotional attachment the reader feels for this character is what keeps them reading.

But how do you get your reader to *love* the protagonist? How do you get the reader to feel that emotional attachment?

Give your protagonist *heroic qualities*.

Qualities that your reader *loves* in the real-life people that *they* love. Qualities to which they will be instantly be attracted.

# **Exercise: 15 min**

1.  Choose someone in your own life that *you* love.
Write down 5 traits that you love about this person.

_______________________________________________

_______________________________________________

_______________________________________________

_______________________________________________

_______________________________________________

2.  Write a paragraph that shows (not tells) your
protagonist exhibiting <u>one</u> of these heroic qualities.
Insert this somewhere in the very first scene
containing your hero.

_______________________________________________

_______________________________________________

_______________________________________________

_______________________________________________

_______________________________________________

_______________________________________________

_______________________________________________

_______________________________________________

_______________________________________________

3.  Make notes where you can insert scenes that display an example of this trait in five other points throughout the first half of your book.

# Day Three: Antagonist

The antagonist is most commonly known as the "bad guy", the character who will try to prevent the hero from succeeding in their goals. But your antagonist is not necessarily the "villain" of the story, they are simply the character who has the *same desire* as the hero.

Remember, the antagonist is the "protagonist" in their own head, even if they do seem to be the "bad guy" as far as the reader is concerned. So you, as the author, must now employ *empathy*. This will allow the reader to (in some way at least) want the antagonist to succeed as well.

NOTE: Sometimes, your story may not have an actual antagonist. Some stories have Circumstance or Fate as the opposing force, rather than a particular character — a metaphorical antagonist. If this is the case, then you need to also create a character who will *metaphorically represent* this antagonistic force.

So whether your antagonist is metaphorical or actual, give them a human soul that the reader will connect with. Make them humble, remorseful, and on some small level, forgivable. Show the reader there may be a possibility that this character could turn their life around, even if it is completely unlikely, because the reader will always cheer on a character who wants to change.

## Exercise: 15 min

1. So *who* is your antagonist?

   First, look at your hero's *want*? Which character (or characters) in your story also wants this for themself, and needs to prevent your hero from achieving this goal? (Can be more than one if metaphorical).

   This person is your Antagonist.

   ___________________________________________

2. Give your antagonist some empathy. Look at your antagonist's *reasons* for causing the troubles inherent in your book.

   What are some reasons that *you* would personally

cause these same troubles, if you had no other choice? Write a short paragraph to justify why *you* would commit these acts. What would drive *you*?

______________________________________________

______________________________________________

______________________________________________

______________________________________________

______________________________________________

______________________________________________

3.  Rewrite the above paragraph into a new scene from your antagonist's point of view, and insert it into your book.

______________________________________________

______________________________________________

______________________________________________

______________________________________________

______________________________________________

______________________________________________

# Day Four: Ally

There will come a point in your book where everything has gone wrong and your protagonist hits rock bottom. They finally realise that their physical goal, the one thing they've been seeking (their *want*), is not what they actually *need* to heal their flaw.

Enter, the ally.

The ally is the one character who will rise up at the last minute and *inspire* your hero to succeed when it all seems hopeless. The ally is the only one who is able to force your protagonist to face their internal flaw, see their core wound, and begin to heal it by seeking what they need: the emotional goal (the book's theme).

They can be your protagonist's best friend who has been alongside them for the entire journey, or they can be a pop-up character who appears in one chapter specifically to deliver this lesson to your protagonist.

NOTE: The ally is an embodiment of the book's theme.

<u>**Exercise: 15 min**</u>

1.  Write a stream of consciousness paragraph about the book's theme.

    Why have you chosen this topic? Why is it important to *you*? Why should it be important to the reader? What do you want the reader to learn because of your book?

    ____________________________

    ____________________________

    ____________________________

    ____________________________

    ____________________________

    ____________________________

    ____________________________

    ____________________________

    ____________________________

    ____________________________

    ____________________________

    ____________________________

2.  Rewrite this paragraph into a speech from your ally, and insert it into your book right before the climax. Have your ally deliver this exact message with as much force and heart as possible.

# Day Five: Narrator

Given that the narrator of your story will be the one engaging with your reader, they need to be someone your reader will enjoy spending hundreds of pages with.

The narrator can appear in your book in a few different ways.

<u>A main character</u>: The story can be told from your main character's point of view, either in first person (I walked…) or third person (he walked.). They are telling their own story and only have access to their own thoughts, feelings, and experiences.

<u>A secondary character</u>: Similar to the above, but although the main plot may not be happening directly to this character, they were somehow a witness and are now relaying the details of their opinion of the events. They only have access to their own thoughts, feelings and experiences.

<u>An Omniscient Narrator</u>: The story is told from the point of view of a god-like character who has access to

*every* character's thoughts and feelings, as well as being a witness to *all* events.

**<u>Exercise: 15 min</u>**

1.  Choose a random chunk of your manuscript, or write out a new scene. Which of the three narrative point of views are you using?

    _________________________________________________

2.  Rewrite the scene using each of the other two narrative point of views.

    _________________________________________________

    _________________________________________________

    _________________________________________________

    _________________________________________________

    _________________________________________________

    _________________________________________________

    _________________________________________________

    _________________________________________________

    _________________________________________________

    _________________________________________________

    _________________________________________________

    _________________________________________________

3.  Do either of the other two narrative types feel more exciting?

# Day Six: Stereotypes

In order to make your characters come alive on the page you need to create characters who are multifaceted, who have flaws, as well as heroic qualities, and are *not* your standard run-of-the-mill character.

To do this, you need to give your reader a little bit of shock value, a little bit of the unexpected, and give your characters a little bit of the uniqueness that we all have within us.

### Exercise

1.  Choose a character. Think about how they're shown to the reader. What are their physical traits, their speech patterns, their quirks?

____________________________________

____________________________________

____________________________________

____________________________________

____________________________________

____________________________________

____________________________________

2.  Write down one way in which this character could be stereotyped?

_______________________________________________

_______________________________________________

_______________________________________________

_______________________________________________

_______________________________________________

3.  What is a contrasting quality to this stereotype? For example, a tough biker type who carries around a fluffy white dog.

_______________________________________________

_______________________________________________

_______________________________________________

_______________________________________________

_______________________________________________

4.  Repeat this for all your main characters.

# Day Seven: Character Types Conclusion

If you've just gone a full week of writing every day, filled out your character profiles, and taken a huge step in fleshing out your current work in progress, well friggin' done! I am *so* proud of you.

And if you maybe missed a few lessons, or not completed the exercises, that's okay too; these practices aren't going anywhere and you can go back to any one of them whenever you want. I am still so proud of you, because you are still here, and you are still showing up for yourself!

Remember, however fast or slow you go is okay. Congratulate yourself for being here in the first place.

So we have now established who each of your characters are.

The protagonist is the hero of this particular transformational arc or journey.

The antagonist is the one wants the same physical goal as the protagonist and therefore will try to prevent the hero from succeeding in achieving their goals.

The ally is the one who will rise up at the last minute and inspire your hero to succeed when it all seems hopeless.

Each character is the star of their own story. They are their own protagonist, they have their own antagonist, and their own ally. Each character has an internal flaw, and a physical goal that they believe will heal this flaw (but won't). Each character has a "need" or emotional goal they will learn, which *will* actually heal their flaw.

Today, we are wrapping up our look into characters by writing out their basic character arcs. This can help to prevent writers block by clarifying directions and decisions that the characters will need to make in further scenes.

Each character will relate to the other characters in different ways, and these relationships will all weave together to form a complex and rich tapestry in your story. Each role is different but necessary for the character arc to be completed.

**<u>Exercise: 10 min</u>**

1.  Using the points we have already looked at over this week, fill out your character arc cheat sheet. For this exercise, look at <u>all</u> of your characters as the protagonist of their own stories, and give each of them their own individual arc, antagonist and ally.

<u>Character Arc Cheat Sheet</u>

Protagonist:

_______________________________________

This character is unhappy because of (internal flaw, example: loneliness)

_______________________________________

_______________________________________

_______________________________________

They believe the only thing that can heal them and solve their current problem is (Physical goal, example:

getting a girlfriend)

_______________________________________

Once they achieve this physical goal, they will realise
that the only thing that can actually heal their internal
flaw, and solve their current problem, is their emotional
goal (or theme ie, self love)

_______________________________________

Antagonist to this character:

_______________________________________

Antagonist Physical Goal (ie, wants the same girl):

_______________________________________

Ally to this character: _______________________________

Lesson for ally to deliver/theme stated:

_______________________________________

2. Fill this out a Character Arc Cheat Sheet for each of
   your main characters

# Day Eight: Reader Connection

As writers, we want to give the reader a reason to care about our characters — all of them. In order to do that, we need to show their humanness. They make mistakes. They want to be better. They hope.

Think of it like a relationship: there's the initial spark, then the honeymoon period, then monotonous life. The relationship will only last if you make an effort to keep the spark alive. It's all about reinforcing the limerence!

How do we do this? How do we make sure the reader stays excited about your characters and your story?

Easy.

Just make sure that *you* are excited about it *when you are writing*!

If you write with an element of excitement, that energy will flow out the ends of your fingers and into the manuscript and then back up into the reader.

As creative people, we have ideas that flit through our minds every day. So what was it about this particular idea that grabbed hold of you and made you start writing. Go back in time. Remember where you were when you got the idea. Remember the inspiration. Remember the feelings that built up within you as you started picturing the characters that would be involved.

Sit in that energy for a beat. And then…

## Exercise: 15 min

1.  Write a stream of consciousness paragraph for each of the following:

    The original story concept excited me because:

    _________________________________________

    _________________________________________

    _________________________________________

    _________________________________________

    _________________________________________

    I need to write this story because:

    _________________________________________

    _________________________________________

_______________________________________________

_______________________________________________

_______________________________________________

I love the character of (protagonist) because:

_______________________________________________

_______________________________________________

_______________________________________________

_______________________________________________

I love the character of (antagonist) because:

_______________________________________________

_______________________________________________

_______________________________________________

_______________________________________________

I love the character of (ally) because:

_______________________________________________

_______________________________________________

_______________________________________________

_______________________________________________

2.  Rework each paragraph to fit somewhere within
    your manuscript's narrative.

# Day Nine: Core Values

The theme you have chosen needs to resonate with *you* personally in order for your story to be infused with passion.

This passion will help you remain excited about your writing.

Although this passion will extend to your protagonist, *all* your characters all will have different reasons and beliefs surrounding it, which will make your book multi-layered.

Let's explore the pros and cons of your specific theme in order to give your book depth.

### Exercise: 15 min

1. Write a paragraph about why this core value / theme is important to *you* (and therefore your protagonist)?

_______________________________________

_______________________________________

_______________________________________

_______________________________________

2.  Rewrite and insert it somewhere in your manuscript
    from your protagonist's point of view.

3.  What is the opposite to this core value?

4.  What are some reasons why this opposite belief is important to others? (Use this as your antagonists' beliefs to challenge your protagonist.)

# Day Ten: Shadow Self

This week is all about secrets.

Every character has something they keep within the shadows of themselves, something they will do anything to keep hidden. In order to achieve their goal and fully transform, they will need to find a way to *accept* this secret part of themselves.

A character's secret is a wonderful hook for a reader if you are able to hint at this very early on, continue to leave little breadcrumbs, but don't actually *reveal* it until late in the story. Humans are a naturally nosey bunch, and they will keep reading if there is a promise of something being revealed that the character does not want brought to light.

But it's not just about secrets. It is also about character flaws. Those parts of themselves they are not proud of. Maybe they have a temper. Maybe a bad habit. It all goes back to the early years, their core wound and false belief. Maybe they were punished as a child because of this, and they have learned they now need to keep this hidden?

But the thing is, in order for the character to fully transform into the person they want to be, they need to accept this part of themselves, and bring it into the light without shame. They need to stop hiding it, and learn to love it.

So, how does a character work through this issue and end up healing it?

They need to become *grateful*.

Gratitude will heal the character. But more importantly, if a character can become grateful for something they were previously ashamed about, then the reader will subconsciously become proud of that character as well. It will deepen the reader's emotional attachment to that character, and therefore to your book.

**<u>Exercise: 15 min</u>**

1.  What is your character's internal flaw?

    _______________________________________________

2.  What event happened in this character's past that
    caused them to feel this way?

    _______________________________________________

    _______________________________________________

    _______________________________________________

    _______________________________________________

    _______________________________________________

    _______________________________________________

    _______________________________________________

    _______________________________________________

3.  What is one reason this character could feel *grateful*
    for this event, in hindsight?

    _______________________________________________

    _______________________________________________

    _______________________________________________

    _______________________________________________

# Day Eleven: Emotion

All stories are written to convey emotion in the reader. But how often is this actually achieved?

One mistake that many writers make is to try and convey a certain emotion by *describing* that emotion. They think that by simply describing the character *feeling* a certain way that the reader will automatically feel that way too. But this is not necessarily the case.

To really smack your readers in the face with an emotional fist, you need to catch them off guard. If your main character has just been left at the altar and is crumpled on the floor in a soggy ball of tears, it is unlikely that your reader will also be sobbing into the pages of the book. Why? Because sorrow is an *expected* response for a character to feel in this particular situation, and subconsciously, your reader will be prepared to protect themselves from it.

You need to sneak up on your reader and throw an emotion at them they are not expecting.

There are different ways to achieve this effect, depending on your direction: go down, up, back, out or sideways.

## Going Down

Every reaction we have in the present comes about as a result of a false belief we learned as a child, that has been buried three layers down. For example, your character may be experiencing envy, because a partner is going away on a holiday without them. But in truth, if you go *downward* and dig through the layers, they are really reacting from a core wound of *abandonment*. Their actual emotion around this is *fear*, not envy. So incorporate this third layer of emotion in your scene, instead of the first layer.

## Going Back

Given that part of the character's healing journey involves overcoming their subconscious false beliefs and core wounds they received during childhood, there will most likely come a time that they will need to revisit this childhood occurrence. Whether this is a literal revisiting, where the character physically returns to the place of their childhood traumas, or just a psychological revisiting where they delve into the depths of their own psyches, the character will need to go *back* in order to finally move *forward*.

When you are writing a scene that involves an emotional reaction, flashback to a time in the character's past where they first experienced this particular emotion, and hint (don't reveal too soon) at whatever darkness they experienced. Remember that revisiting this memory will be difficult for your character, in fact they may even have repressed it. Therefore, going back to analyse why and how this is continuing to affect your character's present day life is going to infuse another layer of inner conflict. Use this to your advantage.

<u>Going Up</u>

Another source of healing can come as a result of spiritual awakening.

The deep need for a character to understand *why* this is happening to them. Or *what* they should have done instead. Or any *regret* they have as a consequence of this emotion.

Have your character's inner emotional turmoil somehow linked in to the *big spiritual questions*: Why is this happening to me? Is this fate? What is the bigger meaning behind this event? What does this feeling epitomise? How does it sum up the meaning of life?

## Going Out

Sometimes less is more, and if you attempt to describe the emotion that is swirling inside your character it will simply fall flat because that is what is *expected*. Instead, use the external world to show all of the emotion in the scene using only the character's actions, or even such things as weather, that can perfectly reflect and mirror the character's inner turmoil by using an external metaphor.

## Going Sideways

Going sideways is where you come at the reader from a completely unexpected direction. Almost the exact opposite of what you are trying to convey.

Example: In my book *Dove*, there is a moment where a young girl witnesses the death of a baby. You would imagine that the emotion felt here would be horror and shock. But in order to convey these feelings, I took it sideways to a whole different level and catch them both — the character and the reader — off guard using an *unexpected* emotion.

*My father carries her past the twelve year-old me in the hallway. Red-faced, he runs with her, his keys jingling in his pocket. They jingle like reindeer bells on a sleigh. And that's when I start laughing. I just start fucking laughing. [She] is dead, and it's Christmas Eve, and it's all my fault, and I'm laughing like the horrific monster I've become.*

By using *laughter* in this scene, rather than tears or racing hearts or clenched stomachs, it makes the character feel disgusted in herself, because surely only a truly horrible person would *laugh* at a terrible time like this. And surely, this revelation is something that the reader would have to agree with. So by coming in from a completely different direction with the emotional punch, the reader is left shocked and horrified after all, even though they had probably believed they had safely blocked that blow.

# Exercise: 15 min

1. Pick an emotional scene in your book, or write a new scene to insert.

2. Look at the emotion that your character is feeling. This is usually the expected emotion, the automatic response.

3. Now turn this around. Rewrite the scene using an unexpected emotion: go down, up, back, out or sideways.

____________________________________________

____________________________________________

____________________________________________

____________________________________________

____________________________________________

____________________________________________

____________________________________________

____________________________________________

____________________________________________

____________________________________________

# Day Twelve: Conflict

One surefire way to heighten reader connection is through the use of internal conflict. Having a character pulled in two different directions at once creates massive tension for the reader.

Conflict can be seen as the good guy battling with the bad guy, that's just a given. But in this case — and in terms of a structural tool that is going to enhance your book tenfold — I am referring to one character who is battling their internal *self*.

Every character has something they desperately want, and this is where we dive deep and use these desires to our advantage. It is now your job as the godlike-writer and omnipresent masochist that you are to analyse what this desire is. To work out what the exact *opposite* of this desire would be. And to then work out how the hell this character can also want *that* opposite desire just as badly. This is where your delicious conflict will come from.

Conflict can be shown in the form of inner turmoil (guilt, fear, indecisiveness, etc.), or it can be from external forces (arguments, fate, weather conditions, etc.). And the best way to create impact is to have both of these forces working against each other at the same time.

Example: my book *Dove* opens with the female narrator, Ray, hitchhiking to Canada with her boyfriend, Japhy, to escape his draft into the army and the Vietnam War. (The arrival of his draft letter is The Inciting Incident). Ray has given up her whole world in order to go with Japhy, and obviously, the thing she wants most at this point is for him to reach the border and safely avoid the draft. Yet, she keeps catching herself guiltily wishing she could stay in the USA, and go to university, and make something of her life.

Likewise, Japhy, a pacifist, doesn't want to fight, kill, or die — hence the reason he is heading for the border. However, knowing innocent people are being injured and killed in Vietnam, and that if he joins the army perhaps he could save some of these people, makes him *want* to go and fight. He then feels guilty and cowardly for running away. These inner conflicts are the basis of every scene in the first half of my novel.

<u>**Exercise: 10 min**</u>

1. Write a list of your character's main five desires.

_______________________________________________

_______________________________________________

_______________________________________________

_______________________________________________

_______________________________________________

2. For each desire, write down its exact opposite.

_______________________________________________

_______________________________________________

_______________________________________________

_______________________________________________

_______________________________________________

3. Write some notes as to how this character can justify also wanting that opposite desire at the same time.

_______________________________________________

_______________________________________________

_______________________________________________

_______________________________________________

_______________________________________________

_______________________________________________

# Day Thirteen: False Beliefs and External Flaw

In our early years, we all develop a false belief based on an event that took place in our lives. This event, and the belief it created, also created an internal flaw. These are like two sides of a coin: the belief and the wound.

Your job here is to subconsciously get the reader to recognise themselves within your characters. If they have a similar core wound that stems from a similar false belief, then they will become invested in how this character might heal themselves — because maybe the reader could take some life notes!

All false beliefs can usually be traced back to four essential roots, or core wounds:

1. Lack: there is never enough … (time, money, support, etc)
2. Safety: it's not safe to … (speak up, be myself, be successful, love, etc)
3. Worth: I don't deserve … (love, happiness, money, etc)
4. Trust: I can't trust … (myself, others, fate, etc)

<u>**Exercise: 15 min**</u>

What are some false beliefs that your character has to overcome:

1.

2.

3.

4.

5.

The opposite of these beliefs are (the true beliefs):

1.

2.

3.

4.

5

For each belief, write down an event that can take place that will challenge each the false belief and make the character realise the *true* belief instead.

1.

2.

3.

4.

5.

Notes:

_______________________________________________________

_______________________________________________________

_______________________________________________________

_______________________________________________________

_______________________________________________________

_______________________________________________________

_______________________________________________________

_______________________________________________________

_______________________________________________________

_______________________________________________________

# Day Fourteen: Reader Connection Conclusion

You've made it to the two-week mark! Well done. How do you feel? You are now officially half way to making writing a daily practice for life.

This week was all about creating a strong connection between your characters and your readers, which therefore leads to a faster paced story that a reader will have trouble putting down.

Today is an Integration Day.

Being our last day on harnessing the reader connection before we move into a different topic, I want you to integrate what you have learned and spend the time working on your work in progress to enhance the emotional connection to your reader by focusing on core values, emotion, shadow self, and false beliefs.

It's all well and good to read books on character development and how to build emotion, but unless you actually put this into practice and integrate it into your writing style, it will drop away.

So go.
Do.
Write!

### <u>Exercise: 15 min</u>

1.  Set a timer for 15 minutes and write a new scene that
    incorporates reader connection with character.

2.  Increase the pace by ending this scene with an
    emotional *slap!* Use this as a chapter ending.

# Day Fifteen: Transformation

Welcome to week three! Look at you go! I'm so proud of you for making time for yourself throughout this challenge. Take a moment right now to look back at the amount of work you have done on your work-in-progress throughout this challenge so far. However much you have done, give yourself credit — it's more than you would have done otherwise, right? And that is something to be proud of.

Okay, now that we have looked at your characters and your emotional connection to the reader, this week we will be looking at the transformative journey that your characters will be undertaking.

Every character in your story will be embarking on a transformative journey. Every significant character will be somehow different by the time they get to the end of the book. They will start off internally wounded, and end up healed. All thanks to you.

To sum up so far, your character has a false belief system that exists deep in their subconscious. Their false beliefs have them to developing certain character flaws that prevent them from living their best life. As your characters move from point A to point Z over the course of his or her story, their beliefs will be challenged over and over again in different ways, until they are ultimately overcome, thus transforming your characters, completing their arcs, and healing their internal flaws.

This week, we will be looking deeper into what it is that your characters *need, why* it is that they need it, *how* they will go about achieving it, and *who* they will be at the finish line.

Today though, I want to look at making these contrasting versions of your character (pre-transformation and post transformation) crystal clear.

**<u>Exercise: 15 min</u>**

1. Write a paragraph that shows who your character is at the beginning.

   Think of it like an opening image. Something visual. Striking. Something that will stick in the reader's mind. A symbolic representation of their flaw. *Show* what it is that they need to heal.

   ________________________________

   ________________________________

   ________________________________

   ________________________________

   ________________________________

   ________________________________

   ________________________________

   ________________________________

   ________________________________

   ________________________________

   ________________________________

   ________________________________

   ________________________________

2.  Write a mirrored paragraph that shows who your
    character is at the end.

    Think of it like a closing image. Something visual.
    Striking. Something that will remind the reader of
    the opening image. A contrasting symbolic
    representation of their flaw. *Show* how they have
    healed, and how they are different.

    _______________________________________________

    _______________________________________________

    _______________________________________________

    _______________________________________________

    _______________________________________________

    _______________________________________________

    _______________________________________________

    _______________________________________________

    _______________________________________________

    _______________________________________________

    _______________________________________________

    _______________________________________________

    _______________________________________________

    _______________________________________________

# Day Sixteen: The Foundation

At the start of your book, you will show the character's normal life, highlighting who the character is and how the false beliefs (unknowingly) affect their everyday life.

Think of them like a caterpillar. At this point, they are oblivious to what they will become, they are just going about their days, eating leaves and getting fat, and maybe a little itchy by how tight their skin is suddenly feeling.

### <u>Exercise: 15 min</u>

1.  Write a paragraph explaining what your character's false belief is during this stage of their journey. Why do they believe this? How does the character's flaw affect them negatively?

________________________________

________________________________

________________________________

________________________________

________________________________

________________________________

________________________________

2.  Rewrite this paragraph in your character's words.

_______________________________________________

_______________________________________________

_______________________________________________

_______________________________________________

_______________________________________________

_______________________________________________

_______________________________________________

_______________________________________________

_______________________________________________

_______________________________________________

_______________________________________________

_______________________________________________

_______________________________________________

_______________________________________________

_______________________________________________

_______________________________________________

_______________________________________________

3.  Insert this paragraph in The Foundation section of
    your book.

# Day Seventeen: The Initiation

After you have established what your character's
normal life is like, something will happen to challenge
this life and their false belief system. This is sometimes
referred to as the Inciting Incident and it is where the
character is faced with a massive decision that relates
directly to their false belief. However, they are
unwilling to let go of it yet. Change can be scary. Stick
with familiar. Better the devil you know.

The caterpillar is being nudged to hang upside-down
on a branch and spin a chrysalis, but the idea sounds so
unnatural and crazy they refuse to do it.

### Exercise: 15 min

1. Write a paragraph explaining how this false belief
   keeps them "safe". Why do they *not* want to let go
   of it?

   ______________________________

   ______________________________

   ______________________________

   ______________________________

   ______________________________

2.  Rewrite this paragraph in your character's words.

__________________________________

__________________________________

__________________________________

__________________________________

__________________________________

__________________________________

__________________________________

__________________________________

__________________________________

__________________________________

__________________________________

__________________________________

__________________________________

__________________________________

__________________________________

__________________________________

__________________________________

__________________________________

3.  Insert it in The Initiation section of the book.

# Day Eighteen: The Breakdown

Because of their unwillingness to change their false belief, the character hits a rock bottom and their world starts falling apart around them. They make mistakes, people leave, they doubt themselves. They finally realise (maybe thanks to an inspirational speech by the ally) that they *need* to change this belief before it's too late.

They are now trapped inside a chrysalis and their caterpillar body begins to dissolve into a soupy-goo.

### Exercise: 15 min

1.  Write a paragraph explaining what will happen to them if they continue to live with this belief system? What will happen to them if they are able to *change* this belief system?

_______________________________

_______________________________

_______________________________

_______________________________

_______________________________

_______________________________

_______________________________

_______________________________

2.  Rewrite this paragraph in your character's words.

_______________________________________________

_______________________________________________

_______________________________________________

_______________________________________________

_______________________________________________

_______________________________________________

_______________________________________________

_______________________________________________

_______________________________________________

_______________________________________________

_______________________________________________

_______________________________________________

_______________________________________________

_______________________________________________

_______________________________________________

_______________________________________________

_______________________________________________

3.  Insert it in The Breakdown section of the book.

# Day Nineteen: The shift

The character tests the waters and makes a decision based on the new "true" belief, rather than the old "false" belief. They face a challenge they would have failed before (or perhaps even *did* fail before) but this time — with this new belief system in place — they succeed.

The soupy-goo made of caterpillar molecules has reformed into a butterfly, and they realise that they now have wings.

### Exercise: 15 min

1.  Write a paragraph explaining how this true belief will heal their internal wound?

____________________________

____________________________

____________________________

____________________________

____________________________

____________________________

____________________________

____________________________

____________________________

2.  Rewrite this paragraph in your character's words.

 

 

 

 

 

 

 

 

 

 

 

 

 

 

 

 

 

 

 

3.  Insert it in The Shift section of the book.

# Day Twenty: The Rebirth

The character sees the proof of how the true belief affects their life. They have learned the lesson. They have overcome their flaw, and are now revelling in the wonder of that.

The butterfly steps off the end of the branch and begins to soar into their new, magical, life — the likes of which they could never have imagined possible at the start of their journey.

### **<u>Exercise: 15 min</u>**

1.  Write a paragraph explaining how grateful they are for this new belief, and this new version of themselves they have transformed into?

______________________________________________

______________________________________________

______________________________________________

______________________________________________

______________________________________________

______________________________________________

______________________________________________

______________________________________________

______________________________________________

2.   Rewrite this paragraph in your character's words.

_______________________________________________________

_______________________________________________________

_______________________________________________________

_______________________________________________________

_______________________________________________________

_______________________________________________________

_______________________________________________________

_______________________________________________________

_______________________________________________________

_______________________________________________________

_______________________________________________________

_______________________________________________________

_______________________________________________________

_______________________________________________________

_______________________________________________________

_______________________________________________________

3.   Insert it in this section of the book.

# Day Twenty-One: Transformation Conclusion

You've made it to Day 21! This is an important milestone for you. According to science, if you have implemented writing into your routine every day for 21 days, you have made it a *habit*. They say now, if you continue this for a further 90 days, it will become a permanent lifestyle change.

This week we looked into how your character will transform through the stages of their journey, like a beautiful butterfly.

On Day Fifteen, we looked at the starting line and finish line for your protagonist by writing their opening and closing images based on their transformation arc.

Today though, I want to build out your antagonist as well.

1. Write a paragraph that shows who your *antagonist* is at the beginning.

   Think of it like an opening image. Something visual. Striking. Something that will stick in the reader's mind. A symbolic representation of their flaw. *Show* what it is that they need to heal.

   ___________________________________________

   ___________________________________________

   ___________________________________________

   ___________________________________________

   ___________________________________________

   ___________________________________________

   ___________________________________________

   ___________________________________________

   ___________________________________________

   ___________________________________________

   ___________________________________________

   ___________________________________________

   ___________________________________________

2.  Write a mirrored paragraph that shows who your
    *antagonist* is at the end.

    Think of it like a closing image. Something visual.
    Striking. Something that will remind the reader of
    the opening image. A contrasting symbolic
    representation of their flaw. *Show* how they have
    healed, and how they are different.

    __________________________________________

    __________________________________________

    __________________________________________

    __________________________________________

    __________________________________________

    __________________________________________

    __________________________________________

    __________________________________________

    __________________________________________

    __________________________________________

    __________________________________________

    __________________________________________

    __________________________________________

# Day Twenty-Two: Glow-Ups

You've made it to our final week! I hope you have swaths of notes, scenes and chapters that you didn't have when we began this journey together. But even if you are only coming out of this challenge with a swirl of new ideas then that is great, too. I'm so proud of you for sticking it out, believing in yourself and making this a new daily habit.

Being a writer always seems exciting at the beginning, when you are first hit with that initial idea and spark and the accompanying surge of *need* to just get writing. You sit down and hammer out a few hundred words, or maybe a few thousand, but then slowly that inertia slows a little, the words stop coming, and you realise that this gig is *hard*. Crafting a piece of art that is 100,000 words long and needs to keep a reader invested for all of those 100,000 words is *hard*. Being a writer is *hard*.

But, just like childbirth, it is also worth it. Your book is worth it. Well done for believing in yourself and for sticking it out.

Today is all about believing in yourself. Today we are going to time travel. We are going into the quantum field…

**<u>Exercise: 5-10 min</u>**

Sit down and write a journal entry. Date it somewhere in the future, maybe in a year's time.

Write about how great you feel because that thing you were dreaming of has just happened.

Maybe you are holding your physical book in your hand, or you just signed a seven-book contract with a major publisher, or your book is being made into a movie, or you received a six-figure advance, or you finally typed those final words: *The End*.

Dream BIG, because big things *do* happen to other people, so why can't they happen to you? They *can*. Trust me.

The important thing is to put yourself in the skin of this future version of you. Feel the excitement. Don't just describe what you're doing, describe who you are *being*.

Try and continue this practice every day. Even if you don't do the journal entries, try and get into their skin once a day and live in that future version of you, feel it, be it, and believe that it is where you are heading.

# Day Twenty-Three: Character Glow-Ups

In order to make your character more three-dimensional, more flawed, more *human*, you need to give them more sides. You need ways to show that they can screw things up sometimes. It gives the reader more ways to identify with them, because hey, nobody is perfect, right?

Give your character a chance to do, say, or think something that is totally *out of character* for them. This will create an element of surprise in the reader and a larger than life moment in your story that will stand out.

### Exercise: 15 min

Take the heroic quality you used in Day Two. What is the exact opposite of this?

________________________________________

1.  Write a short scene in which your character is faced with a situation where they demonstrate this *opposite* quality.

2.  What does the character think about what they have just done/caused, and how do they *feel* as a result?

3.  Give them a reason to *justify* their action.

4.  Give them a reason to *regret* their action.

__________________________________________________

__________________________________________________

__________________________________________________

__________________________________________________

__________________________________________________

__________________________________________________

__________________________________________________

__________________________________________________

__________________________________________________

__________________________________________________

__________________________________________________

__________________________________________________

__________________________________________________

__________________________________________________

__________________________________________________

__________________________________________________

__________________________________________________

__________________________________________________

# Day Twenty-Four: Plot Glow-Ups

The different plot points in your book will also come with certain levels of public and personal stakes. The events will directly affect both your character on an internal level, as well as the world on an external level.

What you need to do here is to make the reader aware of exactly what your character is at risk of *losing*, and why this matters.

By doing this, you will increase tension as well as your reader's investment in the story. This equals pages being turned.

1.  Make a list of all the major turning points and twists in your story.

______________________________________________________

______________________________________________________

______________________________________________________

______________________________________________________

______________________________________________________

______________________________________________________

______________________________________________________

______________________________________________________

______________________________________________________

______________________________________________________

______________________________________________________

______________________________________________________

______________________________________________________

______________________________________________________

______________________________________________________

______________________________________________________

______________________________________________________

______________________________________________________

______________________________________________________

2.  For each one, write a brief paragraph about what is
    at stake for each one. What does your character
    stand to lose? What do they stand to gain? Why
    does this matter?

________________________________________________

________________________________________________

________________________________________________

________________________________________________

________________________________________________

________________________________________________

________________________________________________

________________________________________________

________________________________________________

________________________________________________

________________________________________________

________________________________________________

________________________________________________

________________________________________________

________________________________________________

3.  Rewrite in your character's voice and insert them
    into your manuscript.

# Day Twenty-Five: First Chapter Glow-Ups

Sometimes taking things *away* can significantly improve a book's opening. Imagine a path that is overgrown with bushes and branches. It might look pretty but it is hard to walk though. By thinning this out, the journey will become more pleasant.

Look at anything in the first chapter that might be slowing down the intrigue factor. Anything that revolves around weather effects, description, or scene setting, backstory. These elements can be used a little further in, unless they are being used for a reason that actually *does* create intrigue that is specific to your story.

**<u>Exercise: 15 min</u>**

1. Look at the word count of your first page. Cut this back by 25%. (Either delete or past back in a later scene).

2. Does this improve the pace of the first chapter?

# Day Twenty-Six: Memorable Moments Glow-ups

Having your character quietly *sacrifice* something for another character can create a massive high moment in your book, and also create great reader empathy for this character.

### Exercise: 15 min

Choose a character and something that they dearly love or need.

1. Write a paragraph about what this thing is, why it is so important to this character, why they are grateful for this thing, and what they will lose if they no longer have this thing.

____________________________

____________________________

____________________________

____________________________

____________________________

____________________________

____________________________

____________________________

2.   Write a paragraph in which the character sacrifices
     this thing for the sake of another character.

3.  Write a paragraph in which this other character
    either A) realises what has been sacrificed and is
    grateful, *or* B) they continue on unaware of what
    has been given up for them.

# Day Twenty-Seven: Narrative Voice Glow-Ups

One element that can raise your narrative voice is the use of *strong* verbs. The verb "to be" — I *am*, he *is*, they *are*, etc, — is one area that is underused in writing voice.

For example, you may have written: "he *was* walking". *Was* is the verb in that sentence. If you reduce this back to "he *walked*" it is instantly stronger.

Better still is if you can then bump this up further to use a stronger verb than "walked", something that will also show the reader the way in which the character walked.

For example: he *shuffled*, he *stomped*, etc.

### Exercise: 15 min

1.  Read through an existing scene or chapter and highlight all the "weak" verbs you can find.

2.  Strengthen as many of these as you can to convey the personality or actions of your character in that scene.

# Day Twenty-Eight: What Now?

It looks like you made it to the end. Well freaking done, my friend! I am so so *so* proud of you, and so honoured to have been a part of this month. It is my sincere hope that you have come away from this challenge with a substantial amount if words under your belt, and also a good healthy dose of inspiration to keep up the good work and keep moving forward on your writing journey.

You may be wondering, "So, now what?" Well, if you enjoyed completing this challenge, then I have a few other options for you.

If you want to continue the party, you can try out my other 28 Day Challenges and focus on a specific area of your work-in-progress.

28 Day *Novel Writing* Challenge
28 Day *Story Structure* Challenge
28 Day *First Impressions* Challenge
28 Day *Endings and What Now* Challenge

You can even choose to work with me one-on-one, either through manuscript assessments, editing, or as a book mentor.

Contact me, or view my other books, at my website <u>MHSalter.com</u> or Amazon.

Thank you so much for taking the time to go on this journey with me.

Now, let me remind you that all great writers have something in common.

*Determination.*

The fact that you have put time and money into this challenge, and into yourself, proves that you *do* believe in yourself and you *are* determined to be a published writer.

<u>**Exercise: 5 min**</u>

Stand in front of a mirror and look yourself in the eyes. Place your hand on your heart and…

1.  Make a promise to yourself that you will complete your novel.

2.  Make a promise to yourself that you will carve out time for yourself.

3.  Make a promise to yourself to just *keep at it*.

4.  And make a promise to yourself to *believe* that you are a great writer.

5.  Repeat this exercise *every single day*.

# First Chapter Assessment

Not 100% happy with your book's opening? Not sure why your first chapter isn't quite working? Get your chapter one assessment by M.H. Salter.

Receive an in-depth analysis on what is working well — and more importantly — on what is *not* working, with suggestions on how you can remedy and improve your first chapter.

- The analysis will focus on the first line and first paragraph, as well as the last line and last paragraph and how well these work together to bookend your first chapter.

- It will look at the different types of hooks you have used and how to add more, as well as the themes in your novel's beginning, and any symbols or motifs used in conjunction with this; if there don't seem to be any, you will receive some suggestions on what could work well throughout the manuscript.

- Conflict and pace will be analysed, both internal and external, and suggestions given on ways in which these can both be heightened.

- Prologues, or any use of backstory, will be highlighted to see if this could work better at a later point by enhancing tension in the lead-up to future revelations.

After receiving your assessment via email, you can dive even deeper by booking a one hour zoom call to discuss and brainstorm your novel further, or sign up to a one-on-one mentorship with M.H. Salter.

<u>What others had to say about their Chapter One Assessment:</u>

*"I think it's a wonderful chance for writers to get that push in the right direction. I loved all of it."*

*"Melanie's assessment was warm and conveyed just how fully my first chapter had been read and understood. My novel was at a point where I knew it needed improving but I was out of ideas and inspiration about what to change. I now have, not only ideas, but concrete exercises to help me put those ideas into reality."*

*"I liked how the analysis was grouped beneath headings that corresponded to the [Novel Polishing] eBook. This made it much easier for me to see where the assessor was coming from, and pair it to the advice and activities in the [Novel Polishing] Book and Workbook. There was a good level of detail in the appraisal that left no question that my chapter had been thoroughly assessed. It would have been an apprehension of mine to have parted with my money and not received an appraisal that had taken the time to help me figure out exactly what my first chapter is (or should be) doing. So, thank you."*

Book your Assessment with M.H. Salter now through MHSalter.com or contact Melanie at the.excited.writer.is@gmail.com

# Notes